Abiding Grace

Prayers *for* Later *in* Life

Rupert Bristow

kevin mayhew

First published in Great Britain in 2016 by Kevin Mayhew Ltd
Buxhall, Stowmarket, Suffolk IP14 3BW
Tel: +44 (0) 1449 737978 Fax: +44 (0) 1449 737834
E-mail: info@kevinmayhew.com

www.kevinmayhew.com

9 8 7 6 5 4 3 2 1 0

ISBN 978 1 84867 869 9
Catalogue No. 1501536

Cover design by Rob Mortonson
© Image used under licence from Shutterstock Inc.
Edited by Virginia Rounding
Typeset by Angela Selfe

Printed and bound in Great Britain

For Sarah, as always, and for Michael and Richard

For the Canterbury pilgrims, in whose company
I wrote many of these prayers

Contents

About the author

Rupert Bristow, a Reader in Trinity Benefice, Folkestone, is the author of eight books of prayers for Kevin Mayhew and was Director of Education for Canterbury Diocese from 1995 until his retirement in 2008. He has taught on VSO in Rwanda, was the second Director of the UK Council for Overseas Student Affairs, and then Dean of Student Services at London South Bank University. He has also been a specialist adviser to a House of Commons select committee, edited and written for various educational publications and chaired Kent SACRE (Standing Advisory Council for Religious Education). He is an Honorary Fellow of Canterbury Christ Church University and is currently a governor of East Kent College and a member of the Discipleship and Spirituality Resource Group in Canterbury Diocese.

Introduction

We are all getting older, though of course in our eyes 'later in life' often means 'older than me'. However, I am aware, especially in visiting older people, that priorities do change, physical limitations do increasingly impact on our lives and, yes, our memories sometimes let us down.

I also realise that as we age we are also blessed with a storehouse of good memories, alongside painful recollections, which just don't go away. We may feel that there was once 'a golden age' when things were much better. Is this age's way of preparing us for our mortality? Maybe, but such thoughts are no less real, whatever their provenance.

Our later years also have the benefit of our long experience of the world and perhaps give us more time to reflect on our lives and to explore and develop spiritual aspects which we may have neglected in the 'busyness' of our working years.

So the origin of this book was the thought that there is a need for prayers which help people to meditate on issues, positive or negative, affecting us 'later in life'. These prayers may be used to assist in our private prayer time; at a time of celebration or sadness; or just to give thanks.

I have also included some 'staple' prayers, including the Lord's Prayer, which often mean more to us in our old age than they did when we heard them, and perhaps learnt them, at our primary school, for example – and certainly at our churches, if we attended regularly.

Whatever brings you to use this book, I hope that it will help individuals, churches, and those on pastoral visits (for example, to residential homes) to tap into and reflect the spiritual concerns of those at this special stage in our lives, with all its blessings and challenges.

Rupert Bristow

FOREWORD

by the Baroness Perry of Southwark

Growing old is what happens to those of us lucky enough to get there! It does, though, bring its own unique challenges as well as rewards, and both of these open new chapters in our relationship with God.

Rupert Bristow's prayers bring a wonderful storehouse of powerful words to put our thoughts and experiences to God in prayer. Rightly, the collection starts with celebration. There is indeed much to celebrate as we move to a quieter, more reflective period of our lives, with time to spend with friends and family and fewer pressures of time and work. I love the prayer of laughter, as this is such a saving grace of old age. With these prayers we thank God for all the grace we have been given in our lives.

Later chapters give us the words with which to lay before God in prayer the anxieties, loneliness, guilt and worry that for almost all of us are a part of getting old. We look back over our lives, and regrets, lost opportunities, mistakes made and sins committed take over our thoughts. Here in this book are the prayers to allow us to bring these to God and to ask for grace to release the past, to receive forgiveness and accept it for ourselves.

It would be false not to admit that as we move towards the last phase of life's journey we do, sadly, face bereavement and loss.

My contemporaries complain that too many times we find ourselves attending funerals of former colleagues and dear friends with whom we once enjoyed companionship and laughter. Most difficult of all is the loss of a lifetime partner and soul mate. It may often be that we feel unable to share our grieving with family, whose busy lives flow on. Pouring it out to God in prayer can be the best source of comfort and release. Rupert Bristow has given us the words with which to talk to God about all this, to lay down our grief and receive comfort in our loss from one who knows us and suffers with us.

From days of celebration to the time when we face death, this book gives us precious and beautiful words with which to talk to God about our lives. As one who has reached old age, I welcome this book. I will use the prayers and contemplate their message. I commend it to all who turn to prayer in later life.

Pauline Perry

Celebrating and sharing

Birthdays and anniversaries

God of great milestones on our way,
let us celebrate this significant birthday,
remembering all that we have experienced,
those who have shared many of those years with us
and family and friends who are present and in contact today.
Thank you for bringing us to this day, Lord.
Amen

[...] years today, Lord!
I want to thank you for steering me through all those years,
being with me in times of trouble,
sharing those precious special moments of celebration.
May I be able to pass on gratitude, Lord, for the years.
Amen

Lord of time and space,
today we celebrate our [...]th anniversary.
Let it be a celebration of life itself,
a partnership between your creation and our lives together.
Wherever our path takes us,
we give thanks for leading us here,
as we follow your way, your truth, your life.
Amen

As we join together in special celebration,
let us take stock of our journey together:
how much we have learned
about each other and about you, Lord.
Wherever you lead us,
let us appreciate all that has gone before
and look forward in Christian hope and anticipation.
Amen

Church Membership

Your Church has given us firm foundations of faith.
May we do our best to provide for future generations
by combining tradition and relevance,
blending time-honoured messages
with new ways of putting these across.
Give to our church members today
a new creative mission, in a spirit of truth.
Amen

God of young and old,
I was wrong about the future of your Church.
Do you worry, too, Lord?
Help me and all church members
   to hope more
   to risk more
   to trust more
   to expect more
   ...and to despair less,
through your saving grace.
Amen

Make us aware of the ministry of every member,
showing and sharing with each other
so that we can all participate
in the work and ministry of the Church,
bringing warmth and witness to your love
and caring outreach,
to us and to all people.
Amen

Almighty God, loving Father,
bestow on us a love of worship,
in prayers and praise, hymns and holiness,
teaching and preaching, reading and visiting.
Let us work together under you,
through thick and thin,
supporting our priests and accepting their authority.
Amen

Encouragement

Lord of nurture,
help me in my encouragement of others,
not for my sake, but yours.
Encourage me to know you better myself,
not for my benefit, but yours.
Give me hope every inch of the way,
not for my righteousness' sake,
but to follow your truth and life.
Amen

Let all the world in every corner sing,
an encouragement to all around
for Christian hope to flourish.
May the gifts you have granted us
be put to wider use through gentle promptings
and an appreciation of talent and potential,
giving us confidence to share what we have found,
in ourselves and in others.
Amen

Encouraging Lord,
healer of souls and mender of broken hearts,
everyone wants and needs your love,
even if they don't know this yet.
May my family and friends
share in the search for the one true Lord,
always with us, ready to respond,
if we but turn to you,
through your Son, our Saviour, Jesus Christ.
Amen

May we always encourage others
as we have been encouraged in our own lives.
May we never dampen enthusiasm or interest,
but always channel this in the right way.
Let us use the bad experiences we have had,
seared into our memories and experience,
to steer clear of repeating those errors,
always in love and with you as our helper.
Amen

Faith

Faithful Lord,
as time goes on I want to grow in faith.
But is this because I am older
– or because I have seen the light?
Help me and direct me
in learning more about you;
and take me closer to you
as I search for a living faith
to carry me through the years that lie ahead.
Amen

Lord of meaning and purpose,
give me the drive to develop the faith
that your Son shared with the disciples.
Let me learn from him and them,
through reading the Bible,
hearing testimonies of others who profess the faith,
by reading about the saints,
and by listening to your ministers.
Let me be open to the Holy Spirit at work in my heart.
Amen

God of hope,
may the faith that inspired your Church
be present today, wherever Christians gather in your name.
Let the good news be constantly refreshed,
in our lives and in our churches,
so that young and old alike
are drawn in to know your love
and feel your presence in their lives.
Amen

Almighty God,
restore in me the capacity to grow in faith.
Help me to recapture that desire to know you better
and to renew my prayer life,
through practice and study,
through prayer groups and retreats,
and through seeing your Holy Spirit at work.
May the Christian service of others
and the inspiration of the saints
bring me closer to you.
Amen

Family

Father, Son and Holy Spirit,
we thank you for the gift of family:
the family who nurtured us and brought us up;
the family we may have been fortunate to form;
and the extended family for whom we have responsibilities.
Never let us forget that every family
is part of your own creation,
granted to us by your grace
and precious in your sight.
Amen

Lord of family and friendship,
may we have in our families
the close relationship of real friendship,
alongside the duty of care and expectation of trust.
We ask that in all our ups and downs
you are always there to guide us and to celebrate with us,
while family members give practical help
and show expressions of joy.
Amen

Our God and King,
all the world is made up of families,
the outcome of that creative spark
which you ignited in humankind.
Help us to use that spark of life wisely,
nurturing responsibility and responding positively,
so that yearning can lead to learning
and the risk of exploration be matched with the gift of hope.
Amen

Leading light and family friend,
your tender touch, demonstrated to us through your Son,
has broken down barriers and encouraged a real inclusiveness
    within us.
May we incorporate these qualities into our own lives and
    relationships,
so that our families can flourish,
following your example of tough love
and our desire to do the best we can,
in good times and bad.
Amen

Father of all,
bring to this family the peace and harmony
that I remember when I was growing up.
Somehow the bickering is worse now
and trust seems to be in short supply.
Let us all make strenuous efforts to remain united
and continue talking to each other.
Amen

God of young and old,
we pray that family remains a cornerstone of religious
    upbringing,
an environment where faith is nurtured,
a safe place for questions to be asked
and a springboard for future faith development.
Amen

O God who cares,
let the onset of age in our family, any family,
bring the gift of loving memories of days gone by,
alongside the senior moments
when the whereabouts of the ketchup bottle
seems like a mystery too far.
Let there be give and take
and a love that binds us together.
Amen

God of hope,
send to broken families
   a desire to restore relationships
   a time to talk through resentments
and the will to keep in touch,
whatever the circumstances.
Amen

Friendships

Ruler of all,
you have shown us true friendship
through your Son, his teaching, his healing,
his listening and his loving.
Help us to be a true friend to others,
wanting the best for them,
always being ready to tell the truth in love
and to be there in times of trouble,
side by side, hand in hand.
Amen

God of companionship,
just as the Emmaus Road was a route
of friendship and surprise,
may we relish being taken by surprise
when people we counted as friends,
yet thought we had seen for the last time,
reappear in chance encounters
and friendship is resumed.
Amen

May friendship flourish throughout our lives,
at school and college, at work or church.
While we do not choose our parents,
we do have the opportunity to choose our friends,
though it is through the changes and chances of our lives
that we meet those with a kindred spirit,
to laugh and cry with, confide in,
and listen to.
Thank you, Lord, that you brought us together,
and keep us in contact,
always ready to resume our friendship.
Amen

God of great mercies,
in looking back on friendships forged and friendships lost,
may we put into perspective what those friendships have
    meant to us,
how they have changed our view of the world,
how they brought us new interests,
how they created safe spaces
where we found refreshment and renewal,
and a lasting peace.
Amen

Grandparenthood

God of different generations,
let us celebrate the gift of grandchildren,
the smiles they bring, the hopes they generate.
May we hold back in our concerns
and be generous in our offers of care.
Give us the discernment we have learnt as parents
as we support our children and see their development as parents.
Amen

Lord of all time,
grant us a touch of pride
as our first grandchild is born into your world.
Let the event bring back memories of our first child,
the strength and the fragility,
the innocence and the determination,
the smile and the scream.
Give our children the patience we never had.
Thank you, Lord.
Amen

May we be glad at our grandchildren's Christian names,
however much the choice is not our preference.
Let their names begin to reflect their nature – and honour you.
Grant them the future you would want for them
and let them reach their full potential in all their relationships,
especially with you,
merciful Father.
Amen

When we are asked to look after our grandchildren,
help us to do so readily and willingly,
never with the aim of spoiling them or being too strict,
but showing our love and respect for their free will,
just as you have shown us
through your Son, Jesus Christ.
Amen

Keeping fit

God of discipline and endurance,
sustain in us that power to persevere
in all that we do and promise to do.
Give us the determination to keep our bodies and minds
in a fit state to face all challenges,
both in our daily round and in our prayer life.
Let it be so, Lord, let it be so.
Amen

Help me to keep mentally alert
by testing myself through games and puzzles,
as well as through reading and researching.
Let me never lose my desire to explore
the world of words and music, art and science,
critically but passionately.
Amen

When I think it is no longer necessary to exercise,
push me into doing so, Lord,
so that I can better do your will,
especially in helping others and serving the common good.
May I always seek to go the extra mile
when I am preparing to do your business,
to the standard you would wish.
Amen

O Lord, the source of all energy,
give me the resilience of old age
to prepare myself for anything that may happen.
Keep me alert in body and soul.
Above all, Lord, may I be fit to meet you.
Amen

Laughter

God of joy and celebration,
let laughter be a tonic and a balm,
when in the midst of toil and trouble
something bubbles up which strikes us as funny,
an inappropriate word,
a story well told,
or a moment of silliness.
Let us laugh at ourselves
and encourage the world to laugh with us.
Amen

May humour be at the heart of well-being,
not the punch-line to a bad joke,
but a sideways look at our daily round,
a puncturing of pomposity
and an awareness of the ridiculous;
chaos in the midst of order;
and an acceptance of age as a source of much humour.
Amen

God of surprise,
your Son took risks and made unusual alliances.
He may even have shared a joke or two,
with beggars, blind men, prostitutes and Samaritans.
But his aim was true and his task unaffected.
So too may we look for the unusual in the ordinary,
encourage insight through humour,
and not take ourselves too seriously.
Amen

Pour down on us, Lord,
the love that invites the sharing of stories,
delight in weakness and hubris,
the realisation that the more we learn
the less we seem to know.
Give us rain when we expect sun
and high tide when we expect low tide,
in the sure and certain knowledge
that with you all things can change.
Amen

Legacy

God our refuge and stronghold,
we give thanks for the legacy of your Son,
whose words and teaching,
whose healing and resurrection from the dead,
have been the cornerstones of our faith
for two thousand years and across the world.
Help us to stand fast in that faith
which has stood the test of time
and has guided and guarded us over a lifetime.
Amen

As we think of the legacy we have inherited from our forebears,
may we begin to think of our own legacy.
Will we be remembered for our strength of mind or heart?
Can we say that we have brought up the next generation well?
Have we instilled a lasting faith and a prayerful way of life
to those who follow us?
Help us to reflect on these matters
and, where necessary, bring about an amendment of life
and peace at the last.
Amen

Never let us say we have crossed a bridge too far,
or failed to risk a leap of faith,
through faint-heartedness or lack of faith.
Help us to be bold in our old age
and to think only of how we can honour you
by giving of ourselves to others.
Amen

Lord, our lodestar and plumb-line,
let me take stock of my life,
weighing up the ways I have made a difference
and the ways I have avoided responsibility.
Assist me in making up any deficit
by doing all I can to tip the scale in your favour,
merciful God.
Amen

Love

God of love,
restore in us the capacity to really love:
love you with all our heart, mind and strength;
love one another as your Son showed;
love husband, wife or partner in sickness or in health;
and love family and neighbour,
even if we don't get on with them!
Amen

Lord of life,
loving you is my desire,
cherishing my life-long partner is my wish.
Give me patience in my old age
to make haste slowly
so that I can give my all in due time,
while remaining both spontaneous
and faithful to the last.
Amen

Love is all around us,
in creation, in little acts of kindness,
in your abiding love for us.
However old we are,
however new you are to us,
may we breathe in that love
and breathe out your Holy Spirit,
so that love is all around,
is all around.
Amen

Loving Lord,
help us in our later years
to appreciate all forms of love,
some in abundance, some in moderation.
Bring us physical love where appropriate and possible.
Bring us brotherly and sisterly love without competition.
Bring us unconditional love between father and son, mother and
 daughter
and, by your grace, may we seek to love you,
as you love us.
Amen

Music

God of great sounds and symbols,
as the years creep by, we give thanks for music,
for songs which bring back memories,
for hymns that we learnt at school,
for great concerts captured on TV, DVD and CD,
for opera and ballet performed live.
Let us acknowledge the gifts of composers and musicians
who reawaken our imagination and spiritual selves.
Amen

If music be the food of love,
let us play on, play on and play again,
as we find ways in music and song
to praise your name in love and adoration.
May we grow closer to you
as we are transported by the music of the spheres,
into a spiritual place,
a garden of delights.
Amen

Lord of sight and sound,
as we bring our praises to you,
let me heighten my awareness of your presence
with music which transcends time and place,
which uplifts me and honours you
with the strains of well-being,
the glimpse of eternity
and the still small voice of God,
even in the middle of a desert experience.
Amen

May joy and hope be the well-spring of music,
music that uplifts,
music that reflects our despair,
music that takes us out of ourselves,
but nearer to you.
Let us never tire of songs
that remind us of you, gracious God.
Amen

Pilgrimage

Lord of great journeys,
give me the yearning for pilgrimage.
May I set out on a quest for better understanding,
taking me to places I never thought I would visit,
learning about saints old and new,
and marvelling at your great works.
Let me follow the steps of those
who have walked closely with you
and know that you are God.
Amen

May we open our ears and our minds
as we take the pilgrim way.
Bring us new experiences of old routes,
fresh insights into ancient stories.
May the stories of the saints come alive,
as we tread in their steps
and look through their eyes.
Amen

Let me be alive to learning from the past,
as I retrace the journeys of old,
made by people at the forefront of mission.
Whether in the steps of St Paul,
or in search of the saints of Europe and beyond,
help me to be in touch with their feelings,
their devotion to you and the tasks they achieved
through perseverance, discipline and faith.
May I take heart and renew my commitment to you,
wherever that takes me.
Amen

God of help and hope,
be with us in the latter stages of our pilgrim journey.
Grant us discernment of your will
and obedience to your call
in our spiritual path towards your truth.
May we draw sustenance and insights
from physical journeys to special places
of triumph and tragedy, peace and sacrifice,
where Christians were challenged, changed or martyred.
Amen

Relationships

Connecting Lord,
in all our links, attractions and fears
help us to see the essence of others
in a smile, in a moment of kindness,
or in a flash of temper.
May our instincts guide us
and our trust not be misplaced.
In giving us your Son you showed the way
in opening up our true selves
to those whom we love,
including you, generous Lord.
Amen

God of love and judgement,
pour upon us your life-giving Holy Spirit
as we make our way in your world,
forging relationships of all kinds
through family, work, church and community.
In all may we discern the right approach, the proper way
to enable those relationships to prosper,
always honouring our relationship with you,
the one, true God, who never lets us down.
Amen

Well-spring of all good relationships,
may we always be sure
to take the right first step in establishing relationships.
May persistence in prayer accompany
and enfold any situation we come across,
to make a good situation better,
and a bad situation tolerable.
Let forgiveness be at the heart of what we do.
Amen

God of hope,
just as you never gave up on us,
may we always try to mend broken relationships,
for ourselves, for family, for friends,
but also for strangers in distress,
for people who seek out our help,
and in our yearning for nothing
to keep us apart from you, redeemer Lord.
Amen

Retirement

Lord of rest and renewal,
we thank you that we have the chance
to spend time exploring your world;
to enjoy the company of friends and family;
to read and enjoy film and theatre;
and to spend more time with you,
our provider and protector.
Amen

Sovereign Lord,
reveal to us more of your treasure-chest
of places to see and people to know,
now that we are liberated from set hours of work.
Kindle in us that creative spark
to show forth your Word
in praise and thought and deed,
so that we can do justice to the gift of life.
Amen

Lord of all the senses,
you have enabled us to work for you through others.
Let me now work for you through the choices I make,
the encouragement I give,
the time I devote to family and friends,
and the way I approach the time given to me in this life.
Amen

Let me never forget the good things in life,
even when illness, infirmity or loss
threaten to upset my plans for retirement.
May your plans for me reveal themselves
and make good my wish
to work to your praise and glory
in all that I am able to do.
Amen

Thanksgiving

God of great generosity,
you have showered us with gifts
through your lavish creation
and in sending your Son
to restore your relationship with humankind.
We often take all this for granted
instead of pausing to give thanks,
which we do now.
Amen

Lord of all,
help me to appreciate your saving grace,
the sheer brilliance of your Holy Spirit,
and the great benefits of this life.
Waking or sleeping, let me treasure all that I have experienced,
sharing it appropriately,
savouring it selectively,
and drawing on it often.
Let the mists of time edit but not exaggerate
all that I have gained during my life.
Amen

Looking back,
may we reflect on the remembrance of things past,
the tastes and smells of our youth,
the flavour of loves lost and won,
the pride of parenthood and grandchildren.
We give thanks for all these and much more,
gracious Lord.
Amen

Let me always be grateful for the great variety of languages
    and cultures,
with different insights and culinary delights.
The delicate taste of saffron,
the smell of fresh baguettes,
the gentle art of yoga,
the nod of the head and shake of the hand,
the guessing game for 'thank you' and 'hello'
in the countries visited on childhood holidays.
For these we are full of thanks and praise.
Amen

The Bible

God of Scripture,
give me the will and the discernment
to use the Bible well.
Steer me through the difficult passages
and point me to the positive guidance I need.
If I prefer the New Testament, reveal the prophets to me.
If I normally choose the Old Testament, show me the
    teachings of Jesus.
If I do not fully understand the power of the resurrection,
give me a companion on the Emmaus Road.
Turn me into a Bible person.
Amen

Lord of all faithfulness,
reveal to us the full glories of Scripture,
and not just our favourite passages,
but also challenging books of the Bible,
which test and deepen our faith.
Surprise us with the range and purpose
of the books that you set before us,
especially if we maintain our daily Bible reading.
Amen

Lord,
I find it difficult to remember where to find the famous stories
    of the Bible.
Point me to the right chapter and book
when I search for the appropriate place.
And when I have found your words,
let me savour the story, relish its retelling,
and learn from its message.
Amen

Bring us an appreciation of the little known books of the Bible,
from Esther to Nehemiah, from Galatians to Revelation.
Help me to grapple with meaning and content,
with the help of patient priests and serious scholars,
so that we can build up a total picture
of the book that is written in your name,
Father God.
Amen

Travel

God of great generosity,
you have given us the world to explore.
Give us the will and the capacity to travel through your creation,
honouring and valuing difference and diversity.
But in going far afield and seeing distant lands,
help us not to neglect special places closer to home
– and friends and relatives who live there.
Amen

Extravagant God,
may we both enjoy and preserve your creation,
through careful stewardship and sustainable travel.
As travellers may we respect the culture and etiquette
of the people and places we visit.
As tourists, may we pay a fair price
and buy locally wherever possible.
Amen

Lord of all,
bring to our travelling a humility and wonder
at the means of transport we take for granted,
by land, sea and air.
We thank you for the imagination of inventors;
the ingenuity of engineers;
and the professionalism of drivers, pilots and sea captains.
May travellers we know stay safe
and return restored and relaxed.
Amen

God of great journeys,
as we grow older, help us
to set our sights high in our aspirations to travel.
May we take reasonable risks to see new places,
without being foolhardy or putting others in danger.
Let us remember our age but not limit our ambition.
Amen

Volunteering

O God, who never counts the cost,
enthuse us, we pray,
with the desire to serve you,
without question, without demur,
and out of love and devotion to you.
Give to us, day in and day out,
a servant heart and a listening ear,
in all we do and say.
Amen

May we choose to volunteer
    our time,
    our talents,
    our wisdom,
    our risk,
    our love,
    ourselves,
in the service of the one who came to be the servant of all,
our Saviour, Jesus Christ.
Amen

God of extravagant generosity,
the least we can do with our additional time
is to devote it to studying you
in thought, word, deed and prayer;
so to encourage others in your service
that our churches are rich resources
and our holy places are reservoirs of peace.
Amen

Great shepherd of the sheep.
lead us, in our later life,
to spend time with you,
not only one-to-one,
but in your community,
for the benefit of the estranged and the outcast,
the lonely and the depressed,
whether with the Samaritans
or as a Samaritan,
without fear or favour, or the expectation of reward,
gracious Lord.
Amen

Wisdom

All-knowing God,
teach me wisdom alongside the knowledge I have gained.
Give me reflection where I once rushed to judgement;
let my instinct be true to you;
may I hold back my advice until I have the full picture;
and give me patience to hear the views of others
and show real interest
in how they see the world, your world.
Amen

Your Son was wise from an early age;
help us discern the rightness of something
not because of the age of the person we hear or see,
but through proper understanding and due consideration.
May we be passionate about being objective
and dispassionate in being subjective.
Amen

Lord of light and dark,
bring us to a time of understanding of the relationship
between the different sides of our character:
what makes us find joy;
what brings sadness;
what energises us;
and what tires us.
May we know our limitations
but overcome them as far as we can,
gracious God.
Amen

Create in us, we pray, Lord,
a real desire to show judgement in making choices,
weighing up the importance of meeting a need
and the need to perceive what is important.
Let the principles of justice and equality,
combined with the virtues of courage and consistency,
go hand in hand with increasing age.
Amen

Coping and hurting

Cancer

Lord, let it not be me
who sees the hurt and pain in loved ones
when cancer strikes.
But if it is me,
let me hope and help,
let me pray and care,
let me be alongside,
as long as you are alongside me, Lord.
Amen

Lord of mercy, Lord of love,
release your power and healing grace on [...],
who has cancer of the [...]
Give her/him courage and faith,
courage in receiving treatment,
and faith in the skills of consultants, doctors and nurses,
who have been blessed by you in their vocation.
Above all, Lord, help her/him to cope
and sustain her/him in Christian hope.
Amen

God of ministry and miracles,
we feel for [...] just now,
as the cancer diagnosis sinks in.
Let us all show empathy rather than sympathy,
listen to how she/he feels rather than recount our own
    experiences,
and take care of those who care from day to day.
Let us be sensitive enough to assist with practical tasks,
as well as commit our real concerns to prayer.
Amen

Lord,
I feel awful just now,
awful from the treatment,
awful about letting people down,
awful because I can't do what I want to do.
I know you are testing me.
Let me be up to the task
and face this thing, knowing you are with me,
not just now, but for ever.
Amen

Care

God of compassion,
as we grow older may we share more care and concern,
not only for our nearest and dearest,
but also for those in our church,
in our community and in our world
who deserve our care and attention
and receive neither.
Help us to open our hearts to young and old,
to rich and poor,
and to make your love known.
Amen

Let the spirit of grace and truth
break through the fog of neglect and indifference,
and renew hope in life itself.
We have known and felt the care you show, loving Lord.
Give us the words to speak to those without hope,
so that they may know your comfort and your peace.
Amen

Lord, help me to hold things together
as my eyes let me down and my hearing fails me.
I know I am the same person today as I was yesterday,
but the years have taken their toll.
May I be realistic in my expectations for the future,
but full of gratitude for the blessings of the past.
Amen

God of great mercy,
let the older members of our family reach out to the young
and the younger elements show respect to the older ones.
May we all see the people we really are,
irrespective of youth or infirmity, age or experience,
and may we value and acknowledge the things we can do,
rather than complain about what we are not now able to do.
Amen

Change

Changeless Lord,
help us to cope with change in our later years.
It is not as if we have failed to manage change in the past
– but it is not so easy now.
May I never equate change with progress,
nor oppose change for the sake of it.
Give me a proper appreciation of development and growth,
so that I can adapt and adopt change
that is life enhancing and life affirming.
Amen

God of power and might,
bring on the change that lifts veils and reveals your glory.
Help me to do my best to embrace and rejoice in the changes
which improve quality of life and bring relief
to those whose life has been difficult and burdensome.
Let change bring hope as well as help.
Amen

Help us in our later years
to see that your Son brought change and disruption to daily lives.
May we acknowledge that such transformation is sometimes
    necessary
if we are truly to follow your Way, your Life and your Truth.
May we be open to change that is good,
to change that brings us closer to you, Lord.
Amen

Lord of all,
in all the changes and chances of life
we know we can always rely on you,
the still, small voice of peace.
Your creation has proved adaptable and infinitely resilient
to the follies of humankind and the attentions of the devil.
Help those in later years to appreciate the fruits of change
and absorb the pains of change.
Amen

Dementia

Lord of all hopefulness,
as we become more forgetful
help us to savour every moment – as it happens.
May we appreciate the efforts of loved ones
who try to assist us in jogging memory.
Give us – and them – resilience and patience
when our efforts – and theirs – cause difficulty.
In all this, show us your love, Lord.
Amen

Bring us new ways to worship you,
alongside long memories of prayers and hymns
we cherish and remember.
Let all who care for us
know that their ministry is appreciated.
Give me the words to say 'thank you'
rather than feeling guilty at my loss of memory.
Amen

God of gaps,
help me to fill in the missing bits
when I try to recall your love for me.
You never tire of being alongside
– in mending broken hearts;
– in giving comfort to the bereaved;
– in healing those with anger in their hearts;
– in bringing hope to the least, the lost and the lonely.
Give me the grace to acknowledge
how I have received your blessings
– and will do again.
Amen

Amazing Lord,
when we are with dementia sufferers,
may we put aside the usual responses
to repetitiveness, to forgetfulness, to unexpected reactions.
Bring us to realise that this is yet another challenge,
at an age when communication can be difficult;
and may our love never waver
through the help and mediation of Jesus Christ,
your Son, our Saviour.
Amen

Dependence

Father God,
it is difficult to depend on others,
when for so long people have depended on me.
Help me to remain independent of mind,
even though I can no longer do everything for myself.
Grant me a sense of interdependence
which you have demonstrated in your creations.
May I learn and adapt,
knowing you are my helper.
Amen

Lord of all,
thank you for the gift of dependence,
when independence is a thing of the past.
But give me the grace to know
when I become too dependent on others.
Let me never take for granted
the assistance of family and friends,
who have their own lives to lead.
Yet help me to remember
to give thanks when assistance is given freely,
above all to you, generous God.
Amen

I know I can't have it both ways, Lord.
You know I cherish my independence,
but I have to admit a dependence on others for some things.
May I be aware when I need to concede a bit of independence
for the sake of the peace of mind of nearest and dearest;
and when I need to stand firm
and show that spark of life,
that freedom to choose,
that you have given us all, in your wisdom, Lord.
Amen

Loving Lord,
may I only complain in love,
and give praise where praise is due.
In a world where independence is assumed,
let us acknowledge that, later in life,
dependencies mount up,
on family and community, on church and state.
If people depend on us,
let us take that as a compliment.
If we depend on others,
let us give thanks, to you and to them.
Amen

Disability/Infirmity

God of all abilities,
may we recognise that we all have abilities and disabilities.
As we grow older, may we come to terms
– with increasing difficulties of mobility;
– with particular problems of sight and hearing;
– with memory lapses on names and numbers.
Help us to make the most of exercises, mental and physical.
Above all, Lord, grant us patience and perseverance.
Amen

Long-suffering God,
bring us hope to continue to learn,
even when our physical powers are waning.
Give us the will to do things well
and to strive to use our abilities
to bring hope and pride to family and friends,
and to honour you.
Amen

Bring us awareness of others' needs
– when we are in the public square;
– when we are with family;
– when we are travelling.
May we always seek to do your will
and follow your Son's example
in listening to the marginalised and helping the infirm.
Amen

Healing Lord,
may we always be glad of the things we can do
rather than rage at whatever is beyond us.
As we grow older, may we be wiser in the things we attempt,
in the help we seek, and in the way we respond to our own
    limitations.
May we learn to cope.
Amen

Health

God of healing and wholeness,
may we value and honour our health,
which enables us to enjoy life.
We know we should not take our health for granted,
but we do when all is well.
Help us to acknowledge this
and to give thanks daily for all that we can do,
rather than dwell on what we can't.
When our health gives cause for concern,
may we hear what the professionals say
and take steps to minimise the damage,
always ready to change our way of life
and to await medical intervention when necessary.
Give us a positive mindset
and the will to get better.
Amen

Lord of life,
help me to realise that my health is a blessing, and not a right.
Give me the humility to know when I need help.
Make me conscious of what others have to cope with
and the need for me to have regular checks,
so that I can take the necessary action before I have to.
Thank you, Lord.
Amen

Grant me the good sense to know my limitations,
even though, for my age,
I feel in good health.
I know that inside we all think that we are 25,
but let the wisdom of older age
take precedence over the arrogance of youth.
Bring me common sense, in place of vanity,
generous God.
Amen

Lord of health and hope,
you gave us the gift of life.
Help us to treat that gift with reverence and respect.
But when we are struck down
by illness or accident,
may we respond positively and gratefully,
listening to doctors and nurses,
eating and drinking appropriately
and praying for a speedy and healthy outcome,
if it is your will.
Amen

Hearing And Sight Impairment

All-seeing Lord,
be my eyes and ears as I lose the use of mine.
Give me wisdom and second sight to compensate
– and faith in others who guide me.
May I bring to mind things I have seen and heard
when everything was clear to see and hear,
even if I could not take it all in then.
Let hindsight and reflection make all things clear,
just as you make all things new,
Amen

Grant us, Lord, the gift of coping,
even when our eyesight lets us down
and our hearing plays tricks with meaning.
Help us to be glad of the sight and hearing we do have,
rather than curse the loss of clear sight and sound.
Above all, give us the confidence
to admit our impairments
and compensate as best we can.
Amen

Lord of near and far,
may I always see ahead,
even where I can't see the wood for the trees.
And let me be alert to the far-off sound
amid the babble around me.
You have given us light and shade in abundance
and sounds of every kind,
from early morning birdsong to the cry of the fox at night.
Let me savour all I hear and see of your creation,
extravagant God.
Amen

God of time and space,
as the years roll by, may we use our senses well,
caring for eyes and ears,
actively listening and observantly seeing.
Let us take extra care in listening out for gems,
from small children and from the elderly,
so that we can remember friends and family
at every stage of their lives,
to go alongside photos, DVDs and videos.
Amen

Heart Attacks

Lord of heart and soul,
grant us the capacity to withstand heart attacks
and where possible to avoid them through a healthy life-style.
But let us not judge others
in the event of a friend or colleague having a heart attack.
May we be mindful of the shock they have had
and encourage them back to health
through your restoring power.
Amen

Almighty God,
you helped me through my heart attack,
which I did not expect or predict.
Let this be a warning and a wake-up call
to listen to what my body tells me;
to have checks more regularly;
and to appreciate the dedication of the emergency services
in responding to the urgent needs of the heart attack victim.
I rejoice to be alive,
but seek your help to cope with changes in the way I live my life.
Amen

Lord of life,
help us to understand the thinness of the thread
that links us to life.
Just as we can experience the abundance of your creation,
we know that all can be extinguished in a moment
because of an undetected hereditary condition
or because we fail to treat our bodies as temples.
May we respect your creative purpose
by doing all in our power to live healthily
and encourage others to do likewise.
Amen

Thank you for giving […] a second chance.
May their heart attack make them value life itself,
make them think of the life to come
and live life in a way that honours you,
respecting the one who gave us a second chance
to live in your truth and to learn your ways.
Amen

Loneliness

God of three in one,
in acknowledging you as the Holy Trinity,
help us to comprehend that when I am on my own
I am never really alone, with you as my helper.
Give me the spirit and the imagination
to know you in the silence;
to love you in the peace;
and to be comforted by you in prayer.
I ask this through Father, Son and Holy Spirit.
Amen

Lord of hope and help,
never let me tire of your care for me,
even in the depths of my loneliness.
Help me to use solitude for reflection,
so that the blessings of this life come to the fore.
And may I be more aware
that others are thinking of me and praying for me,
even if they are far away or unable to visit me.
Give me the desire to use technology to improve communication
and to avoid using technology as an excuse not to make contact.
Amen

Lord of stillness and silence,
make me grateful for every effort
that others make to maintain contact.
Help me to rebuild relationships that have faded,
especially my efforts to know you, Lord,
knowing you have never given up on me.
Thank you.
Amen

Generous Lord,
you have granted us the gift of relationships.
Help me in my interaction with others,
so that I may truly know, and show, both respect and
    appreciation.
Put me in others' situations
as I seek to bring authenticity to my efforts.
Let me express my appreciation of others
through shared interests, not forced friendship.
Show me a better way to grow
– and to love you more, too.
Amen

Pain

God of great resilience,
you know what it is to suffer pain
through your Son's agony on the cross.
Grant us the strength to absorb hurt and pain,
and the suffering of loved ones and friends,
as well as our own injury and sickness.
May we know your comfort
and be sure of relief from pain,
through your Son, Jesus Christ.
Amen

Hold us, Lord, in the palm of your hand,
as we wrestle with pain
and seek relief in medicines and treatment.
If it be your will, free me from suffering,
through the healing hands of others
or through the miracle of your love.
Let us not limit our hope of relief
by assuming nothing can be done,
as all things are possible with you,
loving Lord.
Amen

Lord of life,
we know that life is not always easy,
or full of celebrations and love and contentment.
May we not feel down-hearted or in despair
when through sickness or accident
we encounter pain, whether physically or in our hearts.
Help us to bear all this with fortitude
and with a faith that acknowledges your great powers,
of hope, forbearance and love.
Amen

God of great powers,
you have through your grace
given us many years of life – so far.
You have seen our hopes and heartaches,
our achievements and our failures,
and you have loved us unconditionally.
In this period of hardship and hurt for me,
keep me in your continuous presence
and lift me from despair to devotion,
as I hold fast to the transforming import of your love for me.
Amen

Strokes

God of mercy and vulnerability,
look on those who have suffered from a stroke.
Help them to regain lost senses,
the capabilities we take for granted.
Grant sufferers patience and the will
to persevere with all the exercises prescribed.
May the body remember and reconnect,
just as many of us have done with our faith,
after neglecting the spiritual in ourselves.
Amen

Lord of tenderness and calm,
just when I thought I was well
I now have to cope with a stroke,
as well as increasing old age.
There are times when I feel it's unfair,
but with your help I know I can recover.
Give me the determination to see this through
and not to make a fuss.
Thank you, understanding friend and Saviour.
Amen

Grant to all stroke sufferers
the art of seeing a glass half full.
Whatever senses and skills have been temporarily impaired,
sight, balance, speech or writing,
may sufferers give thanks for the senses unaffected,
for the blessings of life,
even if it is not the abundant life we are used to.
May carers show understanding
and families show responsibility and love.
We ask this through Jesus Christ.
Amen

God of trial and purpose,
let strokes test our resolve
to recover our faculties,
with the help of doctors, nurses
and specialist medical practitioners.
May this joint effort pay off
in gradual healing and patient rehabilitation.
Give us the gift of hope,
so that we can see this through together, Lord.
Amen

Technology

Let us give thanks for the advances in technology
that make things so much easier than before,
especially as we increasingly struggle to do the 'heavy lifting'
  of old.
Please, Lord, why did it take hundreds of years
to add wheels to suitcases?
And stair-lifts and escalators make moving around so much
  easier!
Also, visiting friends and family across the globe
is now a real option rather than a forlorn hope.
May we appreciate these things – and be glad.
Amen

Lord of imagination and spirit,
give me insights into using technology to your purpose,
from researching prayers and sermons
to looking up daily readings or my favourite poem.
Grant me the will to overcome my stumbles,
by trial and error,
but also by listening to those who know more than I do,
however hard that may seem.
Amen

The things that I need most just now, Lord,
are patience, patience and more patience.
Why can't I do what I used to be able to do?
I just don't understand technology enough,
but I know I need to take it seriously.
Never let me be afraid to consult the young on these matters
and channel my frustrations into practical applications
of that technology to help me adjust to my limitations,
if it is your will, gracious Lord.
Amen

God of all hopefulness,
let our reliance on technology never deflect us
from our hope for a future with you,
in this life and the next.
May we grow in trust,
even as we grow in faith.
May our faith be strengthened,
even in our own increasing vulnerability,
as your Son's was.
Amen

Remembering and worrying

Confessing/Saying Sorry

God of forgiveness,
in our later years we look back with the benefit of hindsight.
We confess to having got things wrong
at various points in our lives.
We are sorry for hurt we may have caused
and wrongs we have committed.
We earnestly seek your forgiveness and hope for mercy
through your Son, Jesus Christ.
Amen

Merciful Lord,
I so wish I had come to you sooner,
but I was too proud to admit wrong-doing.
As I get older I see that I treated [. . .] badly.
In asking you for forgiveness,
help me to say sorry to him/her too.
It's not right to fall out for the rest of our lives,
when through your love
we can make all things new again.
Thank you, Lord.
Amen

Grant me, Father, the strength of humility
and the gift of vulnerability,
especially as I share my sins with you.
May I be aware of the effects of my behaviour
and seek to make amends, wherever feasible.
If it is too late to do that for some,
I place myself before you as a penitent sinner
to do with me as you will,
long-suffering Lord.
Amen

God of night and day,
I used to see things very clearly in my mind,
but I'm not so sure now.
Please assist me in my uncertainty
and make me better able to discern your will for me.
May my faith deepen as I get older,
even as I grow in appreciation of diversity
in expression of faith.
Amen

Debt

Redeemer Lord,
we are always in your debt
for the lifting of the burden of our sin through your Son.
Grant that we, in our later years,
may seek to lift the debt of future generations,
avoiding profligacy and malpractice,
always upholding the principles and practice
demonstrated by the ministry of your Son,
our Saviour, Jesus Christ.
Amen

Generous God,
let me not store up treasures on earth,
but be careful also not to run into debt.
Help me to be a wise steward,
but also share any wealth I have
with those whose needs are greater than mine.
Let me be ever mindful of the needs of neighbours near and far,
as well as family members going through difficult times.
May I never be poor in spirit.
Amen

God of judgement and wisdom,
may my trust in others reflect your trust in me,
but in the knowledge that some people will let us both down.
Help me to err on the side of generosity,
but only in the knowledge
that we should love our neighbours as ourselves.
Amen

God of mercy and justice,
later years bring joys as well as heartaches.
Grant us the ability to meet our debts
as well as show our gratitude,
to family, church and friends,
hoping for a legacy that makes a difference to future generations
and avoids passing on a burden rather than a blessing.
Help me to be sensible as well as sensitive in response to need.
Amen

Golden Age

Lord of the years,
grant to us fond memories of good times,
without claiming a 'golden age'.
May each generation have its own great milestones
and its own advances in science and technology.
But never let us believe
either that past generations were better
or that progress is inevitable.
May we meet the challenges of the future,
not rely on past glories.
Amen

Create in us a right perspective on the decades of our youth.
May we appreciate the positive experiences,
regret our youthful excess
and appreciate the wisdom gained in later years.
May we relish and value our later years,
with reduced responsibilities but greater opportunities
for serving you and leaving a good legacy
for future generations.
Amen

Lord of past and present,
may the amazing grace of your great love
linger in our memories, as time goes by,
and sustain us in the way we approach our later years.
Let us not make comparisons,
but enjoy what comes our way,
especially the joy of grandparenthood
and the challenges of caring or being cared for.
Amen

God of hope,
bring me the consolation of belief
as I struggle with my faith.
Help me to believe that a golden age is to come,
not lost in the rose-tinted mists of yesteryear.
Let me look forward in trust
and backwards with thanks, faithful Lord.
Amen

Guilt/Shame

God of forgiveness,
help me to overcome any sense of guilt
which makes me feel that I have let my family down.
Let me make amends for the selfish decisions I made
and for the harsh words I may have uttered.
Bring me fulfilment in these efforts
so that I can make my peace with them
and with you, merciful Lord.
Amen

Lord of justice and mercy,
you know my inmost thoughts,
my feelings and motivation.
Give me the self-knowledge
to understand the effects of my actions
and the ability to say sorry – and mean it.
I feel guilt and shame in admitting my faults
and trust that in my later years
I can be open and forgiving to others,
as well as to myself.
Amen

God of truth and light,
shine your laser beam of mercy
on my transgressions and wayward behaviour.
Grant me the humility to accept my shame
and the Christian hope to seek amendment of life
as I confess my sins and open out to you,
ever-loving Lord.
Amen

All through my life, Lord,
I have tried to be top dog,
always eager to take the lead.
Rein me in, Sovereign and Saviour,
so that I only seek to serve you,
following your ways and proclaiming the good news,
not for my sake, but yours.
Amen

Loss

God of love and sacrifice,
you know the pain of loss.
Help me to come to terms with mine at this time.
Let me grieve without despairing
and mourn without regretting or forgetting.
May fond memories gradually take the place of tears
and your hope bring comfort to hurt.
Amen

Lord of life,
our loss is hard to bear
and we cannot take it all in.
Help us both practically and psychologically
to make the correct arrangements
and consult the right people.
Let us put it all into your hands
as we worry and fret,
but be ready to accept the help of both family and friends
at this difficult time.
Amen

God of community,
may we rekindle the bonds of community
in responding to the effects of loss.
May [...] be remembered for all that she/he was
and all that she/he still means to us.
Let his/her foibles be recalled,
alongside the skills and gifts that now are lost.
And make us think how we are better people
because of his/her impact on us.
Amen

Grieving God,
just as your Son wept at the death of Lazarus,
so may I be allowed my tears
and not hold back my grief.
But let me also know I have a friend in you,
as Lazarus did.
Give me hope that we will meet again
because of your promise of salvation to those who believe.
Amen

Memories

Omniscient God,
you are always the first to know
and the last to forget.
Grant us the gift of fond memory
and the blessing of selective forgetfulness.
But may we always remember faces,
even if names slip from our grasp.
Give us the good grace not to get upset
if others forget our names
as they look into our souls.
Amen

Lord of majesty and memory,
may your love and mystery
always remain in our hearts and minds,
while place names elude us
and Christian names challenge us.
Help us to cherish our memory,
not curse our ever-increasing 'forgettery'.
Amen

Merciful Father,
in our later years
let us rejoice in the long memories of times past
when our children were children
and our grandchildren were future dreams.
We thank you for the things that were
and the things that were to be,
by your grace.
Amen

God of purpose,
our memories have a reason,
just as our imagination gives us hope.
In looking forward,
help us to learn from looking back.
And in all that we do
may we recognise that our actions
begin, continue and end in you,
sovereign Lord.
Amen

Regrets

Lord of forgiving,
let me not harbour thoughts of what might have been.
Rather bring me gratitude and joy
for all that has made you glad.
Let the fond recollections
take the place of regrets for missed opportunities.
Help me to understand that all life is learning
and regretting is part of that process.
Amen

All-seeing God,
take away the bitterness of regret,
as I pray:
for those I could have helped but didn't;
for those I didn't try to understand;
and for those I listened to but did not hear.
Create in me a better awareness
of my weaknesses and others' strengths,
knowing that you are there to steer me.
Amen

Gracious God,
forgive my heedless actions
which may have caused hurt or harm.
In seeking your understanding, Lord,
let me strengthen my resolve
to seek reconciliation with others
and peace within myself
so that regrets can lead to repentance
and restoration can lead to renewal.
Amen

Lord of recollection and risk,
May I always take risks for you,
sure in your love and protection.
Let me never be afraid of regrets,
if the alternative is only to attempt
those things which I feel I can do without help.
Nothing I achieve and nothing I experience
can be without the abiding grace of your creation.
Amen

Remembrance

God of love,
at Remembrance time may we think of those of our relatives
who paid the ultimate sacrifice
– in conflicts near and far.
Grant me the perseverance
to find out more about their lives and deaths,
valuing every fact and every story.
You know the pain of loss.
Help me to treasure the gift of memory.
Amen

Lord of life and death,
in the midst of life may we acknowledge death,
the manner of it,
the purpose of it,
the value of it.
May I recognise and better understand
the notion of an honourable death
in defence of freedom and country.
At this time help me make time
to know how and why people in our families and communities
gave their lives for a greater good,
and wonder at their sacrifice.
Amen

Thank you, ever-giving Lord,
that young people remember those who have gone before.
Let us not be surprised
that the stories of the past
can affect and influence the young today.
May we play our part
in encouraging research and providing information,
to make the past come alive.
Amen

God of infinite memory,
help us in our later years
to remember those who meant so much to us in earlier times,
from real-life heroes to comic book favourites,
from brave men and women involved in war-time heroics,
to acts of courage and thoughtfulness in our daily lives.
Let us give thanks and be glad.
Amen

Remorse

Lord of wholeness and healing,
deliver me from feelings of remorse
which have dogged me over the years.
I keep on wondering
whether things would have turned out better
if I had been more honest with loved ones,
more demanding of authorities
and more involved in religious observance.
If praying is about holding people up to you,
I lift myself up before you,
ready to come clean and make amends,
ready to turn over a new leaf with you,
if it be your will.
Amen

Bring me relief from remorse;
grant me a second chance to restore relationships;
let me love myself again;
bring me hope;
change me.
Amen

Remind me, Lord,
that you know me better than I know myself,
in my going out and my coming in.
Grant me a resolution to my remorse,
so that I can put bad things to one side.
I know now that I had misplaced loyalties and unworthy goals.
Bring me a new start
through staying close to you,
and witnessing to you in all I do.
Amen

Almighty God,
may your amazing grace transform my life,
even though I am set in my ways.
Give me a new lease of life,
through seeing others cope with distress.
Let me acknowledge and put aside those hidden resentments,
all those bitter, unresolved disputes.
Make everything new
so that I can turn my life around
– towards you.
Amen

Story-telling

God of New and Old Testament,
you know how to tell a good story,
including, some say, the greatest story ever told.
I pray that the younger generation
may be captivated by the stories you tell
and that they will carry them into their later years,
as I do.
Amen

Thank you for the gift of story,
so loved from early years to the third age.
Encourage and inspire story-telling,
to continue to imagine and retail
stories which baffle and bemuse,
stories which bring laughter and tears.
May we never lose the capacity
to be carried away by stories well told,
adventures and romances which involve us
and triumphs and tragedies which move us.
Amen

Lord of mystery and imagination,
give us in our later years
that same capacity to wonder
we had in our early years.
Whether we are telling stories
or listening to romantic tales of derring-do,
may we get caught up
in the power of a tale well told.
Amen

God of glory,
you have placed us in this part of your creation,
free to live and move and have our being.
Grant us courage to explore and explain,
so that we can enhance that experience,
as well as help others to fulfil their potential
for flights of fancy
and great exploits of the imagination.
Amen

Worry and Despair

God of hope,
as I get older I do worry,
not about my own future,
but about my family and friends.
Help me both to let go
and to encourage others in their development.
May my errors and omissions be warnings to others,
but also a reassurance that all can be well,
by your grace.
Amen

Lord, I despair at worry
and worry about my despair.
Release me from this vicious circle.
Help me to concentrate for a few seconds
on the good things of life,
the blessings I have received . . .

Then help me to set against these blessings
the bad things in life . . .

May I discern how to counteract the latter with the former,
with you at my side
and in my heart, Lord.
Amen

Encourage me, Lord,
to worry not and want not;
to see a glass half full;
to replace pessimism with optimism;
and under your careful watch and bountiful care,
to give you thanks and praise
always and in all ways.
Amen

God of love and life,
bring your abundant generosity to bear
on my great capacity to worry.
When I am prone to despair,
wake me up to your glory.
Whenever I think that, as I grow older,
only bad things happen,
remind me that I really do
have God on my side,
as your Son came to show us,
without fear or favour,
and with a servant heart.
Let me serve, too, Lord.
Amen

Planning
and hoping

Downsizing

God of time and motion,
may we face facts
and realise that our need for space has reduced.
Give us the will to take action,
to re-order our affairs and reduce our belongings,
so that others can move in
and we can re-locate
to a home which fits our needs
rather than our wants of yesteryear.
Amen

God of justice and fairness,
help us to adjust to our situation,
recognising both our needs and our limitations,
our means and our age.
May the hopes and dreams we had when we moved in
be replaced by a new realism
which acknowledges that our spiritual well-being
does not depend on objects,
but on a right relationship with you,
our Lord.
Amen

Lord,
we know that small is beautiful,
but sometimes we don't act as if we do.
May we not be proud or protective
in hanging on to what we have.
Grant us the generosity and honesty
to let go of things that may be better used by others,
even if it is the house that has been our home.
Thank you.
Amen

Bring us a sense of proportion
in an age of excessive wealth and excessive poverty.
Help us act to make this a reality
in the way we lead our lives today.
Give us purpose in our choices
and may we be governed as much by the needs of others
as by the imperative of making do.
May our small steps bring focus to us
and help to others.
Amen

Funerals

God of beginnings and endings,
help me to cope with the funeral ahead;
give me strength to support family and friends;
grant me time to grieve;
and let fond memories replace tears,
as we lay […] to rest.
Amen

At this time of life
I seem to be going to lots of funerals:
old friends stricken by illness;
elderly family members fading away;
and people seemingly in the prime of life,
carried away by random accidents and violence.
Help me to find meaning in all this,
so that I can help others cope
as well as retain my own Christian hope.
Amen

Lord of resilience,
give me the strength to play my part in [...]'s funeral.
May I reflect on and share
how she/he made a difference in our lives.
Let me be true to his/her spirit
and the impact she/he had on the lives of others.
May I do justice to a life which we experienced
and a soul you are welcoming into your heavenly kingdom.
Amen

Great shepherd of the sheep,
just as your Son taught us
to go the extra mile for the lost sheep,
empower us to care for the least, the lost and the lonely,
especially at the end of their earthly lives.
Give us the heart and the will
to acknowledge the spirit of each life,
shaped by you and shared by us,
and may we ensure that the funeral of anyone,
great and good or lonely and unloved,
is done with dignity, grace and an understanding
that everyone is special in your eyes,
redeeming Lord.
Amen

Hope

God of great expectations,
prepare us in Christian hope
for the journey ahead:
the years left to us here on earth;
the promise of the life to come;
and the transition between the two.
May that transition be as natural as it can be.
But I do worry about the process,
not least for those left behind.
Be alongside us the whole way, Lord.
Amen

Lord of love,
grant us the hopefulness we see in the lives of saints.
As we grow older,
may the flame of faith burn brighter,
as a lamp to lighten our path,
but also as a beacon to others,
to show the extraordinary in the ordinary,
the holy in the humble, we pray.
Amen

Let hope loose wherever it can breathe.
Let optimism be the light,
faith be the taper
and your love be the candle.
May all these banish the darkness of despair
and the blackness of pessimism,
even as we grow older.
Amen

Amazing Lord,
create in us we pray
a heart for you;
a hope in you;
a helping hand to you.
Grant us in our later years
a sense of your peace;
a sense of your presence;
and a sense of your purpose for us
in all we do in your name.
Amen

Letting go

Almighty God,
who always holds us close,
help us in our later years
to let others take up the baton,
not in order to give us an easy life,
but for the future well-being of those we serve.
And not just amongst family and friends,
but in the communities and organisations
dear to us and in which we have invested time and energy.
May we let go – and let fly.
Amen

Give us the grace to let go,
even when people ask us to stay.
May we have the wisdom to know
when others have more creative ideas
and the energy to see them through.
We have your Son's example in sending forth the disciples
to do his work and spread your Word.
May we have the humility to encourage others
to do better what we have begun.
Amen

God of time and place,
let us know when it is time to let go.
Create in us the judgement
to know when to give others the chance to flourish
in areas we thought were our own.
Thank you, Lord.
Amen

Sovereign Lord,
direct our hearts and minds
in the task of keeping the flame of faith alive
by sharing your Word,
but also by sharing our tasks,
even when we think we can still do them better ourselves.
Let us know our limitations,
as well as our potential – and that of others.
Amen

Life after death

Eternal Father,
we know you have promised those who believe
a place in your heavenly kingdom.
I worry, Lord, about whether I have enough faith
– to trust without anxiety;
– to convince others that this is true;
– to stand before you in confident hope.
Help me to be a good witness
to your unfailing love
and unbroken promises to humankind.
Amen

Grant us a glimpse of eternal life
in our experience of your creation,
whether in a flower in bloom
or human nature engaged in your work.
Give all those who believe
and are not long for this world
the assurance of your saving grace
and an awareness of your presence in our lives;
so that we can all seek to make
the seamless transition from life to death
without fear or regret,
but in confidence and trust.
Amen

Lord of all time,
let our brief spell in this life
not be the end.
Some of us have been fortunate to enjoy a long life,
even a full and rewarding life,
while the lives of others have been cruelly cut short.
Let all who trust in you,
and perhaps others by your grace,
have the opportunity to know what is to follow
when our time comes.
Thank you, Lord.
Amen

Gracious God,
will I see again, face to face, those who have gone before
when I enter into your eternal kingdom?
If so, may I have the humility
to acknowledge the influence of others
and to give thanks for all the things
which I now know were precious and special,
to me and to you.
Help me to cross the bar in hope and expectation.
Amen

Mentoring

Almighty God,
in all that we learn in life
your Son is our mentor and our friend,
equipping people to help us grow
in love and knowledge of you.
May we in turn be of help to others,
if we are able, with your support and inspiration,
to be mentors to others in their faith journey
as part of our own ministry.
Amen

Great shepherd of the sheep,
as we seek to find our way in our later years,
we know we are called upon
to be pastors to others along the way.
Equip us, we pray,
through learning from our peers;
through reading scripture and psalms;
through prayer and fasting;
through peace and quiet;
and with you ever present in our hearts.
Amen

Ever living Lord,
grant us the gift of growth in our knowledge and love of you.
But also make us hungry
to bring Christian hope to others.
Let us journey together,
as on the road to Emmaus,
you at our shoulder,
us eager but sometimes unaware.
Expose us to the full potential of our relationship with you,
so that we too can walk alongside others
and help them to see the light.
Amen

Liberate us, Lord,
from ignorance and self-satisfaction.
Whatever we have been able to achieve
is only through your great mercy.
Prompt us to mentor others
in sharing whatever gifts we have to offer.
Make us good mentors and partners with you,
in all you want for us.
Amen

Moving

Lord of everywhere and nowhere,
as I come to move house,
let me reflect on this place,
the family home where we have been happy,
the garden where we have played and partied,
the neighbours we had, now moved away.
May our next move be a wise one
and bring us in contact with new people,
while remembering the friends we have made here.
Amen

God of homecoming,
may we value the home we have had,
but look forward to moving to a smaller place.
Help me to redistribute things I no longer need
and only keep what I really require.
May my Bible be always at hand,
so that psalms and gospels
can punctuate my day
and I can live and work to your praise and glory.
Amen

Loving Lord,
as we move, may our hearts remain with you,
as we go to a new place, may we make a new home;
and as we say goodbye to this home,
may we always be in your house,
wherever we worship you
and have our being.
Amen

Lord of life,
may our living always revolve around you,
wherever we find ourselves,
wherever we rest our head.
Give us the grace to accept new ways,
new neighbourhoods, new places,
and new people to get to know,
as long as we remain rooted in your love.
Amen

Saying goodbye

Lord of welcome,
help us to say goodbye well,
to others who move away,
to friends and family who go to be with you
and find it hard to let go.
May I learn from those who do this well,
so that when my time comes
I can do so with hope in my eyes
and peace in my heart.
Amen

Lord,
I know that it's hard to say goodbye, then say hello.
But over my life
I know that goodbyes well done
can herald new beginnings
and generate fond memories.
May I remember this – and be glad.
Amen

Amazing grace you show to us,
unmerited love you give to us.
Let that unbroken bond of pastoral oversight
survive every goodbye along life's road.
And for every fond farewell,
may your welcome shine through
and bring us home.
Amen

Lord of greeting and hope,
you have showered us with blessings aplenty
and experiences of a lifetime.
Grant us the chance to say our goodbyes properly,
to friends and neighbours, when we move on;
to loved ones when they pass from this life to the next;
and when it is our turn,
to take that leap of faith
– into your loving arms.
Amen

Stepping Down

Empowering Lord,
you showed the way to trusting others,
especially your Son, to do your will.
When the time comes for us
to step down from job or position,
may we do it well and with grace.
Give us the faith to let go
and the humility to praise our successors
whenever praise is due.
Thank you, Lord.
Amen

Leading light,
shine your bright beam on the path before us,
so that we can step down,
confidently and graciously,
knowing that you will support us along the way
– and catch us if we fall.
Give to those who follow after us
the same encouragement and support
that you have shown to me,
ever present Lord.
Amen

Lord of power and might,
you have shared that power and might
with your Holy Spirit, your Son and his disciples,
right through to us today.
You have given us a purpose
and made us a strong link
in the chain of discipleship.
Look on us now as we step down
and give us hope for a future in you.
Amen

You have given us hope and a trusting soul.
As I take the next step,
help me to remember those who went before:
the way they encouraged me;
the way they let me learn the hard way;
the way they handed on the baton.
May I do them justice – and you proud.
Amen

Taking on

Tireless Lord,
I am told that retirement is a job for a younger person.
Equip me, I pray,
to be useful and helpful,
even when my main employment is over.
Give me a servant heart
and an intention to say 'yes',
but may I also know my limitations
in seeking to do your will.
Amen

Lord of constant watchfulness,
give me enthusiasm and stamina
to follow things through
when I take them on.
Let me never say 'yes'
without offering a prayer.
Let me never say 'no'
without offering a prayer.
And let me never fail to bring anything significant
in prayer and supplication to you.
Lord, let me be your prayer partner.
Amen

Almighty God,
time and again I take on too much,
never wanting to say 'no'.
Please, Lord, guide me in my decisions.
May I take things on for the right reasons,
not because I am flattered by the request.
Give me perseverance alongside willingness,
a determination to go with aspiration
and follow through with application.
Amen

Trusting Lord,
you have taken me on through your Son.
The least I could do is take things on for him.
Guide me into the right actions,
as I am called upon to serve.
Whatever I do for you,
I do willingly and gladly.
For all that you do for me,
thank you.
Amen

Wills

Let it be that I can know that
my will is your will,
full of hope and help,
thanks and trust.
Whatever I have received
has come from you.
Whatever I leave
you have given me.
Let me be wise and fair,
in allocating that part of your creation
over which I have had temporary stewardship.
Amen

Lord of all,
help me to be wise and timely
as I come to update my will.
Let me not forget
all those who have helped me,
not just those to whom I have a duty of care.
Banish any residual meanness or favouritism,
and let me show in my will
that I have learnt from your grace and generosity
in this life,
as I prepare for the next.
Amen

Settle my mind, Lord,
as I make my will.
Settle my heart, Lord,
as I order my affairs,
Settle my will, Lord,
in doing your will.
Settle my soul, Lord,
in giving it to you.
Amen

Lord of night and day,
may I have peace of mind
when my time comes,
knowing I have served you;
knowing I have hurt you;
knowing I have been forgiven by you.
Let my will reflect
the faith you have nurtured in me
and the judgement you have forged
in my mind,
but also in my soul.
Amen

The Lord's Prayer

Our Father, who art in heaven,
hallowed be thy name;
thy kingdom come;
thy will be done;
on earth as it is in heaven.
Give us this day our daily bread.
And forgive us our trespasses, as we forgive those
who trespass against us.
And lead us not into temptation, but deliver us from evil.
For thine is the kingdom, the power and the glory,
for ever and ever.
Amen

or

Our Father in heaven,
hallowed be your name,
your kingdom come,
your will be done, on earth as in heaven.
Give us today our daily bread.
Forgive us our sins as we forgive those who sin against us.
Lead us not into temptation but deliver us from evil.
For the kingdom, the power, and the glory are yours,
now and for ever.
Amen

A general thanksgiving

ALMIGHTY God, Father of all mercies, we thine unworthy servants do give thee most humble and hearty thanks for all thy goodness and loving-kindness to us and to all men; We bless thee for our creation, preservation, and all the blessings of this life; but above all for thine inestimable love in the redemption of the world by our Lord Jesus Christ, for the means of grace, and for the hope of glory. And we beseech thee, give us that due sense of all thy mercies, that our hearts may be unfeignedly thankful, and that we shew forth thy praise, not only with our lips, but in our lives; by giving up ourselves to thy service, and by walking before thee in holiness and righteousness all our days; through Jesus Christ our Lord, to whom with thee and the Holy Ghost be all honour and glory, world without end. Amen.

The Book of Common Prayer